TEARS, CHEERS & FUNNY Stories

BY LYN BETAR

COMPOSED BY
MISH MOCKOVIC MARTIN

BALBOA.PRESS
A DIVISION OF HAY HOUSE

Balboa Press books may be ordered through booksellers or by contacting:

Balboa Press
A Division of Hay House
1663 Liberty Drive
Bloomington, IN 47403
www.balboapress.com.au
AU TFN: 1 800 844 925 (Toll Free inside Australia)
AU Local: 0283 107 086 (+61 2 8310 7086 from outside Australia)

Print information available on the last page.

ISBN: 978-1-5043-2272-0 (sc)
ISBN: 978-1-5043-2273-7 (e)

Library of Congress Control Number: 2020919200

Balboa Press rev. date: 09/29/2020

There would be more than two in the room at any time. She knew how to draw a crowd and hold their attention. In all honesty, it was she who made them feel good rather than the opposite. She was quick to a joke perfectly themed to any given conversation, and her ability to give rise to a smile, a sneaky chuckle, or a deep belly laugh was obvious by the mood in the room.

The room was filled with ready-to-bloom Tahitian lilies, prized for their long stems and large flowers, boasting a profusion of feminine scents rich in ginger and lime, sweet and lingering in a purposely sterile room. Complementing the lilies were gerbera daisies, happy and cheerful, offering energy and positivity. The arrangement had sprinkles of yellow carnations, also rich in colour, to bring forward the notion of enlightenment and intellect.

A vase full of red roses stood on the sideboard, contributing to the array of colour. The petals, delicately wrapped around fragile buds, emitted an aroma that one could almost taste, like a good wine. Traditionally, red roses are a symbol of love, an expression of emotion, but their soothing, anti-inflammatory, and mildly astringent properties make rose petals ideal for healing. The long-stemmed beauties express balance and the promise of new beginnings of health and longevity, which everyone in the room was hoping for.

In that moment, not many words were spoken. They were simply being in the moment and appreciating the now. The past that could not be changed held memories for everyone there, memories of time spent together over the years, more than a century shared when one considered the age of each, each with his or her own recollection of events and places unforgettably joyful and pleasant.

It is true: the power of words singularly spoken or scribed can have an influential force on an individual. Words can be beacons of inspiration, enthusiasm, and encouragement when expressed with kindness and respect. Words can soothe your soul, melt your heart, bring a tear to your eye, or place a lump in your throat. They have the power to evoke the splendour of your emotions that can heal, help, and humble. Thich Nhat Hanh, a contemporary Buddhist monk and global peace worker, writes that the spoken word should always convey respect, gentleness, and humility, regardless of content or differences.

Words can completely change your life, and this can be true of what is to follow. A collection of poems collated over five decades that reflect raw and honest emotion from the poet who once said her life was ordinary but extraordinary. Some poems are mirrors to her soul, baring all, exposing true thoughts and feelings in a vulnerable manner. The time was 1975, not long after a divorce, which back in the day was a very controversial issue, especially with the church, which incidentally had been legalised earlier the same year.

The words will touch you deeply, and you will know the poet—if not before, then by the end of the book. The style and format were deliberately chosen to weave poems around people, places, events, and time, first starting with the poet.

The poet's mum was born to Margery Valentine "Marj" Cotter and Colin Fredrick "Fred" Taylor in the same year the Second World War ended, thus making her arrival auspicious to those she endeared. But she was also one of the first baby boomers, a stereotype of the people at that time compared to the generation known as the millennials.

Marj and Fred lived in a flat in Clovelly, and Marj used to talk fondly about this time. Although trams gave her terrible motion sickness, they also gave her freedom and access to the city—something she had not experienced in Wetherill Park. However, as a toddler, my mother nearly fell out of the window of the flat, so they decided it wasn't safe to live there anymore, and they moved back in with Marj's parents, Bertha Grace Cotter (née Sanders) and Frank Cotter. This must have been so difficult. Frank was an alcoholic, and Bertha Grace wasn't a very happy soul. It was never sure whether she was naturally grumpy or whether Pop's alcoholism had caused her to become so. I can't imagine that this was a time of unbridled joy for the young family either. There was this notion that the firstborn should be male, so in the eyes of the Cotter family. Mum had committed a fatal sin by being born female. However, my grandmother was determined not to allow that shallow mentality affect those she loved, and she made sure my mother didn't feel less important or valued than her brothers. I recall my grandmother being tiny but feisty, and it would not have surprised me if she was one of the first liberators, like the suffragette Vida Goldstein. The Cotter men could be difficult at times, and for that reason alone, a good, strong woman was required in the family to tame their autocratic ways.

Their place of residence was set on six acres, and despite Frank's alcoholism and taciturn nature, he had the most beautiful garden. It was full of bird of paradise and chain of hearts and was a truly magical place to be. It was always hard to reconcile the man with his garden. He lived in a sleep-out on the veranda of the house. There were only four other rooms: the kitchen, the dining room, and two bedrooms. I guess it must have been quite a squeeze.

My grandfather, who become fondly known as Fred, and his brother Max were offered work in the family butcher shop, called Ice Works and Slaughter Yards at Narooma. Trying to build a relationship with a father who had been absent for much of his youth was a waste of time because Arthur Baden Marcus Taylor was a heartless man. One case in point was when Fred cut the sinew in his thumb and was made to catch the bus one hour to Moruya Hospital for medical attention. What kind of father does that?

Mum tells the story of being taken out to the slaughterhouse with her dad when she was five. No doubt she begged to be able to go with him. He, being a hardened, old bushy, probably gave in and took her. For Megan, her younger sister, this was a traumatic event, especially in the eyes of a six-year-old. Her being forced to carry rabbits as they bled all over her cardigan after a killing spree was never a fond childhood memory. In fact, I have it on good authority that Megan has never eaten rabbit or kangaroo to this day due to this incident.

Likewise, there was time that Mum was playing in the grounds of the slaughterhouse and happened upon Fred shooting a cow in the head with clinical accuracy. That was a momentous event in her life. Mum ran away before being noticed, and Fred was never aware that she'd seen. It affected her deeply, and as an adult, she has been an advocate for animals, rescuing all shapes and sizes over the years. She became well-known as the crazy cat lady. I think she may have coined the expression. For Fred, it was a necessary evil—eat or be eaten was his motto—but for a five-year-old, it must have caused considerable trauma.

My grandfather was in Moruya Hospital for six weeks, and fortunately there was compensation in those days. Once discharged, Fred had to put his mended thumb to work by hitchhiking home. It reminds me of the classic *Hitchhiker's Guide to the Galaxy,* and for poor old Fred, his experience was out of this world. He owned a motorbike, which blew a piston at Kiama. He managed to get the bike on a goods train that was leaving the following day. Without a mode of travel, he started to walk and got as far as Mt. Ousley, where he hitched a ride to Central Station and caught a train to Fairfield. Then he walked four miles to home. Quite the epic journey and a great story to be told because there were no apps in the day and no Uber on standby.

The motorbike in question must have been the one my grandmother spoke fondly about. It had a side car that accommodated her and Mum, both wrapped in blankets against the gruelling wind while travelling to Burragorang Valley (before it became a dam) for picnics. It was always hard to imagine my grandmother in a sidecar, with or without a baby!

While still on compensation for the injured thumb, Fred got a job on a horse and bread cart, which lasted four months. Once the funds were received, he bought a GMC logging truck. They continued to live with Nan and Pop when Colin was born, and Fred logged out of Oberon for about seven years. Five acres at Wetherill Park was purchased thereafter, and an old weatherboard house from Fairfield was transported to the block to establish a new life and family home. A brickie from Lancashire was hired to complete the works, and to this day, no one knows how the house got build because no one could understand his accent. But it was completed, and I remember the dwelling well, especially being chased around the kitchen table by my uncles, swimming in the above-ground pool, and finding out I was allergic to bees when stung in the ear. I loved to play dolls with my aunty Megan, who was only six years my senior. She had a sewing machine and made beautiful clothes for them. I was, and still am, in awe of Aunty Megan because she introduced me to pizza.

Years later, I was perhaps fourteen when Megan and her gorgeous boyfriend, who was the hang glider for the Blue Stratos commercial, asked me to dine with them at Pizza Hut.

After working for a butcher in Smithfield for many years, Fred sought more security and gained employment with Prospect County Council, where he worked until he retired. He was a disconnection officer to start with and then became an investigation officer for the recovery of bad debts. He certainly met a lot of interesting people in his travels. There is a poem dedicated to Fred, and much of this information will resonate when read.

Fred was quite the personality, and he and my mother were very close. In fact, those who knew him loved him. When he passed, there wasn't a dry eye in the room, and I was surprised to hear how many people's lives he had touched with his kindness and warmth.

He was a proud, hardworking man and always had time to listen. Material possessions were not this man's worth because one can't measure a person in these terms, but he did like to collect "valuable items," or as my grandmother would say, "junk." He built sheds to house these items, and the sheds were fun to explore, almost like the forbidden closet in Narnia.

It was a pretty rustic life. The toilet was a pan, but there was no "dunny man" to empty it and take it away. That was Fred's job, and he had to take it and bury it on the property. It was a long way from the house, and there was a path lined with yellow cassia shrubs. There were many wet or creepy midnight treks to the toilet. The laundry was also a free-standing building with a wringer washing machine; once wrung, the clothes were like pressed cardboard. Snakes visited both of these places from time to time to make life more interesting.

The house had a fuel stove, so there was a lot of chopping wood for the fire. Fred would get telegraph poles delivered, and these would be sawn into chunks. I hope they were not for inside use and saved for the epic bonfire nights that my grandparents used to host. They were amazing. It would take months to build the bonfires, and everyone would come. The bonfires would be full of old logs, trees, and tyres. It was environmentally inappropriate, but apparently they were the highlight of the year. We would attend as a family, and my dad, who had recently trained in hypnotherapy, hypnotised a number of the neighbours at bonfire night. "Just look into the fire and stare, and listen to my voice," he would say. Mum was a bit anxious about that, and poor little Matt was too scared of the crackers to join in the fun; he stayed in the house with my grandmother. She would make a huge vat of pea and ham soup that was as famous as the bonfire.

The wood stove in the house was an institution, and even when an electric stove was installed, the old girl was put to use. It meant there was always a kettle boiling, and the wood box underneath provided warm comfort for any injured animals. It was used to save all sorts of animals: puppies, kittens, possums, and birds.

My mother always had a love for all creatures grand or small. There have always been horses and consequent falls. There is the old saying "Get back on the horse again," and she did. Mum competed in a few competitions as an adult, receiving ribbons for her performance. I'm not sure whether the news of a spider in her riding jacket or her reaction to it was the reason she won first place at Dubbo Show, but it certainly made a good yarn.

Wetherill Park was an untidy, eclectic five acres. There were dogs, cats, pigs, goats, chickens, sheep, and of course a horse. Tucked away in the outer west of Sydney, it was kind of isolated but always full of life. My grandmother used to describe it as like Ma and Pa Kettle's, and for those old enough to remember those movies, you'll understand the ambience. For those not old enough, it was a bit of a shambles, but that didn't matter. They were surrounded by Italian market gardeners who generously shared fresh fruit and vegetables; that provided an international flavour to meals and valuable friendships.

The house was no mansion, and it was a rustic way to live. At the age of sixteen, while attending Parramatta High School, my mum left the farm to live with her soon to be husband and his family in Blacktown. That's where I come into the picture.

Of course, we didn't meet until January 1966. Our first meeting was fraught with concern by the doctor on duty. I was experiencing anaemia and suffering jaundice caused by the antibodies from the mother's blood. It wasn't the best introduction into the world, but that didn't stop us from being close.

I had an adventure-seeking spirit, always in search of fun, and digging holes in the garden looking for diamonds or chasing rainbows to find the pot of gold was a daily activity. I kept my mother busy. I would love to play school, always choosing to be the teacher because I had a willing student. Tedious and boring as the games may have been, she never failed to be excited and fun to be with. I loved to dance to Daddy Cool, and I listened to the Little Gingerbread Man on vinyl—records that Mum bought home after working the night shift at RCA Records. I started school earlier than anticipated—not because I was exceptionally academic but because the little school at Wetherell Park needed student numbers to fill the classes, otherwise a teacher would have been transferred. From this point onwards, I noticed I was a little different from the other kids. I was different not in looks but in the way I was dressed and by the contents of my lunch box. While others were enjoying a Vegemite sandwich, I had cut vegetables, nuts, and grains. Always an advocate for healthy, nutritious foods, my mother was different from others—something I was to appreciate later in life.

Being force-fed broad beans, a legume I loathed, wasn't the happiest experience in the memories of a five-year-old. This happened the day I was taken from school by a mysterious person. Like any other day, I was walking out the front gate on my way home when a car suddenly pulled beside the foot path, and I was grabbed and shoved in the back seat. No seat belts were required in the day, but I recall the burning sensation of the car seat covered in fake leather and the sting of the metal buckle on the strap. Driving to an unknown address, I had no idea where I was and who the people were. They were certainly not unkind in any way, but seriously, any self-respecting kidnapper should probably provide a feed of fish fingers and Fruit Loops to gather compliance from a kid or a bribe of chocolate or lollies, but definitely and wholeheartedly not a plate of broad beans.

The reasoning behind the abduction was due to a failed marriage and trying to find a safe haven for the interim. Once reunited with my mother, all of this was explained, including the broad beans, and I knew it was going to be an extraordinary life and not an ordinary one.

My parents met in the Flamingo Coffee lounge, a chic café in the suburbs that celebrated delicious pastries, cakes, and sandwiches, with freshly grounded coffee filling the atmosphere already heavy with conversation. The layout of the establishment was always a talking point. The floor was tiled in large red, black, and white sheets in a chequered design, the chairs and coffee tables were the original retro before retro became trendy, and the hero in the room was a wall dedicated to painted flamingos standing at the watering hole. Wait, there is more! The ceiling was a tapestry of rope and bicycle wheels, a feature unique to the shop. A Wurlitzer sat in the corner, popular with the teenagers who frequented the café on Saturday afternoons.

One of those teenagers was my mother. She represented Parramatta High School in netball, a feisty goal defender, and after the game (played in Fairfield), her friends would customarily visit the Flamingo Coffee lounge to celebrate their wins. Ordering a frothy cappuccino at the counter, friendly banter would take place until eventually an invitation to the drive-in theatre was accepted. Actually, truth be told, it was a group date. Harry was to accompany my mum, and Harry's sister was to attend the movie with my future dad.

By the end of the evening, a new relationship unfolded. Let's be clear: it was not between Harry and his sister. As a result, the news of a baby the following year. My mum worked in the café throughout the pregnancy, wearing stiletto heels, which came in handy; more on that later. She had a flamboyant style, and her image was similar to the icon Dusty Springfield, with teased bouffant hair, thigh-length hems, and heavy eye make-up that made her look like a movie star.

Often customers of the café would comment that Mum looked similar to Audrey Hepburn from the movie *Breakfast at Tiffany's*, something I would attest to. She definitely was a natural beauty.

The Flamingo Coffee lounge was a popular watering hole with several biker gangs, especially after midnight. This one particular evening, a banded group of leather-clad fellows arrived to dine after a night of partying. Fuelled with alcohol and issues with diminished height, one of the bikers became aggressive and confrontational with my father, who politely asked the group to leave.

A few pushes and shoves ensued, and my dad was seriously outnumbered. When things started to go pear-shaped, my mother, who was witnessing the sequence of events unfold, came from behind the counter, heavily pregnant in high heels and wearing a minidress. The combination of the heels and hair made her appear taller than normal but definitely taller than the surly biker. Without any hesitation, she removed her shoe and cracked the unknowing fellow over the head. Blood poured from the wound, dripped down his forehead and into his eyes, and mixed with embarrassment and sharp angry tears. He eventually left, only to return with more leather-wearing guys.

Ready to pounce and cause havoc like Russell Crowe in *Romper Stomper*, they saw the offender: a heavily pregnant woman. They were confused at first because it was hard to understand the extent of the injury to the man's face when comparing the size of the attacker, but when common sense kicked in and it was clear the wounded fellow was a nancy, bouts of laughter filled the room, thus breaking the tension.

The years in the café had its moments, but for the most part, there were happy times. This was before the golden arches, fast food outlets, and shopping centres consumed and engulfed the suburbs. The streets were once lined with small business owners like the Flamingo Coffee Lounge on Swanson Street. Across the street was the Council Chambers, next door was a florist, and down the way was Joe, who owned the local fruit store with tomatoes the size of apples. Often one would hear Joe shout, "Pomodoros, come and get your pomodoros," which added character to the neighbourhood.

My dad was a good provider and a successful businessman, and my mum would want for nothing, but the age difference and cultural separation strained the marriage. After ten years, a few fur coats, and a brand-new mini, Mum decided to leave in 1972 before divorce was legalised. It takes a lot of courage to leave the security of a home and marriage. An intrepid that knows no bounds, she set of into the wild, which in Australia is beyond the Great Dividing Range—metaphor intended to describe the events that took place. The wild was lush, rolling green hills surrounded by deep valleys and volcanic-rich soil to establish a new life under a different name.

In her new-found freedom, Mum had so much fun fulfilling every whim from disco dancing lessons to clothing parties and playing squash, which unfortunately is a non-existent sport today because squash courts are commonly replaced with treadmills and gym equipment. That needed to be said because I didn't want you to think she was playing with vegetables, but in all honesty, it wasn't the sport she enjoyed; it was the wine afterwards.

She was employed at the local psychiatric hospital in the medical records and came to know the patients well. Many had huge personalities, or several, and were endearing characters with interesting lives. In fact, Mum would often comment that it was hard to distinguish between the patients in the hospital and the general public; in her opinion, there were more crazies outside the walls of Bloomfield Hospital than within.

In a small country town, the news of her divorce spread quickly, and as such many suitors came to the front door to ask her out. In the quest for her attention, she received many gifts, including slabs of meat—hence the repeated expression "Lamb is the new lobster." We ate well. There were helicopter rides, offers to remove dents from the old green Torana, a puppy, and even a job offer to manage a fast food chicken shop. This one caught her attention, and after three months of intense training in Carusla, a suburb in Sydney, she was promoted to manager with a company car.

The company car was an average station wagon, but in someone's good humour (most probably a marketing ploy), there was a chicken head attached to the roof. It definitely defined the car and driver when cruising the streets, but what made it especially noticeable was the forward and backward jolting movements of the head when the car changed gears. It had a seriously long clutch, perhaps ten inches above the floor, and to the innocent onlooker, the chicken looked more like Woody Woodpecker than a tasty chicken dinner with peas and gravy.

The decision to work in fast food was a good one because the love of her life entered the doors of Big Rooster to purchase a chicken roll. He did so on any given Monday, but on this particular day, he was served by the manager. Taken by her beauty, he asked her out for a drink, to which the reply was, "If I had drinks with all those who'd asked, I would be an alcoholic." He left without his roll.

It is said persistence is a quality more valuable then intelligence, and in this case it is true. After declining many invitations to share a beverage, mum finally accepted the chicken roll man's offer. In preparation for the date, she took great care with her appearance, styling her hair, applying make-up, and choosing a white dress with lace. They shared prawn cutlets, salad, and a bottle of red. At the conclusion of a wonderful evening, they both declared mutual affection for one another. I guess when you know, you know.

I was constantly in strife for taking the chook mobile without asking; probably it was something to do with company policy. I doubt it was because I wasn't a licensed driver. More than once, Mum received a phone call from the police to politely ask if I wouldn't take the car, or at least if I would come to the station and sit the driving test. I mention this because back in the day, one would call into the local cop shop and ask if someone was available to take a learner for a driving test, which involved a hill start, a three-point turn, and a reverse park. I passed with flying colours, though admittedly I had had loads of unsupervised practice. The kind sergeant issued my piece of paper, which one could doctor to get into pubs and clubs underaged, on the condition Mum got the seat belts fixed. Those were the days.

I was an easy child to parent and didn't cause my mother many worries. One time, I said I needed money to buy fabric for a debutante dress, a tradition in the country to announce young ladies to society. I got announced but spent the money on a 1972 Ford Escort—yellow in colour, so it was hard to miss. One would have thought that purchase would have pleased those involved, because I didn't need to take the chook mobile without asking, but it wasn't. Another time, I decided to drive to Surfers Paradise without permission. I simply got in the car and kept driving north. I guess it could have gone unnoticed except the need for petrol money to return home. "Return home from where?" was the question. The money I received by a bank wire was well spent on accommodation for a further six nights, food, and partying, with just enough funds put aside for fuel to travel twelve hours home. The decision to enrol me into a Catholic Ladies college that was once a convent was apparently easy.

Our time in the country was eventful, and Mum always wanted to leave the town in a white Mazda sports car. A little romantic, I suppose—the whole thing about being "rescued" by a knight in shining armour. She was rescued, in a manner of speaking, by the chicken roll man, who did eventually buy Mum the car of her dreams, but we left town with all our belongings, Sam the cat, and Georgie the silky terror (remember the gift of a puppy) in my Ford Escort.

Country living must have suited Mum. After a decade in the city in a house on the stunning Sydney Harbour, they moved to Dubbo after purchasing a Toyota dealership. A five-year plan extended fivefold, and after twenty-plus years, Mum had plenty of material to compose poems. You will note the tone and style is significantly different because most of the written word was on people and places.

You will also notice her sense of humour for which she was greatly endeared.

The poems beautifully note major events such as weddings, birthdays, and even funerals. The mechanics in the garage, the sales team on the floor, and the receptionist at Dubbo City Toyota didn't escape her wit.

The time has come to sit back, relax, and enjoy the beautiful collection of poems that describe the feelings and thoughts of the poet. The collections of words uniquely placed in stanzas have their own rhythm and time—a time well remembered with tears, cheers, and lots of laughs.

CONTENTS

MIRROR OF YOUR SOUL

I am the mirror of your soul.
Mould me with your mind.
You only see perfection
When love has made you blind.

If you never look beyond
The adoration of your eyes,
I will never disappoint you
With the cruelty of lies.

Our nights will be all velvet,
And days of golden sun.
Night and day will mould together,
And heaven will be one.

Let the now be ever-present.
May I always walk with pride
In the warmest glow I've ever known
Because I'm by your side.

April 20, 1975

GOSSAMER WINGS

Down in the limitless depths,
I would wonder a short while
To weed the garden of my dreams
And find peace to smile.

A prisoner without prison clothes,
A prison without bars.
But once again incarcerate
With different wounds and scars.

Oh, hear my voiceless prayers,
Longings without utterance.
Give my spirit gossamer wings
To catch the wings of chance.

This mortal span will soon be through,
And with the setting of life's day.
In reflection of a life misspent
Not one noticed I passed this way.

April 20, 1975

THE MASK

I have walked today in the shadows
And cast fast-held values aside.
All that is constant is endless change.
Behind what mask do I hide?

Do I cling steadfast to an empty ideal
When I have laughed in its face with derision,
Or grow without pain the knowledge I've gleaned
And look at my life with new vision?

Have I learnt today what I needed to know,
That one never knows oneself truly?
To accept the growth that every day brings
And never judge anyone cruelly?

Time and youth will pass away.
How swiftly they slip by.
In the winter of your life,
Don't let the beauty die.

Please remember me always
As you think of me tonight.
Never allow this rose to die;
Nurture it and keep it bright.

And when I am remembered,
I will truly never die.
Whisper my name for the wind to carry,
To echo through the years gone by.

May 5, 1975

EVENING SONG

You won't pass my way again.
I know that this is true.
I wish you health and happiness
In everything you do.

Please don't say goodbye to me.
I know our interlude has passed.
The sweetest love I have ever known
Is just a memory from the past.

And when you are far away,
Spare me a stolen thought.
Remember me as I am today
In memories in close rapport.

Don't look back in sadness,
No regrets for yesterday.
Recall the beauty only.
We knew we could not stay.

Dreams have faded with the night,
And death comes on the morn.
I cannot face the evening song,
Laugh away the scorn.

I've sung my song all out of tune;
I couldn't dance the beat.
The only round I ever won
Was that of dull defeat.

I won't be noticed passing,
Not even simple sights.
For the dance that never danced,
No uttered faint goodbyes.

July 2, 1976

GOD'S GRACE

Too many years have come and gone,
Too many winters have passed,
So many sunsets in the west
Since I saw you last.

Too many tears till none were left
Have dried upon my face.
How many buried memories
Grown sweeter by God's grace,

I know now you've shared my sadness
Though our paths went separate ways.
True friendship's tie will never die
In the winter of our days.

Don't look back in sadness;
The past is beyond recall.
But each new day in its special way
Holds the dearest hope of all.

June 14, 1978

MINDLESS MADNESS OF MACHINERY

Many the ways the feet can tread,
Many the hearts that are weary.
Featureless faces half blend with despair,
Cling to a life that is dreary.

To drink a drink to industry,
To drain your glass of misery.
To the mindless madness of machinery
And snore above the roar.

Hands that are set each day in motion,
Minds that have long lost their reason,
Stumble each day in a robot-like way
That alters not with the season.

April 1978

TIME

Oh, most elusive quality,
You can be friend or foe.
Healer to the aching heart,
Torment when you love one so.

You no longer bother me
Because I no longer care.
I can be alone without you
Because no one else is there.

So while you are my company,
Teach me to use you right.
Help me to be happy
And keep the spark alight.

If my one returns to stay,
He'll find there will be no needs
Because absence has estranged us both.
Love does not grow like weeds.

July 8, 1976

THE MEANING OF LIFE

Life is far too serious.
We mostly miss the mark.
What's happen to the humour.
And the lighter side of dark?

Where's the joy in living?
The glorious morning song?
A friend's arm on your shoulder
To say you belong?

When we do for everybody,
We don't count the cost.
Open up our hearts and home
For any soul that's lost.

And are we grateful that we may be
In a blessed state,
And often soften heavy loads
For someone we call mate.

How sad our little worlds become
About what we leave behind.
What's happened to a handshake
And trust side of our mind?

Ah, our good Lord in heaven
Must wonder what to do.
But if he doesn't see it my way,
I'll see his angles too!

STRANGERS IN THE NIGHT

The firelight flickers on the hearth,
The shadows rise and fall.
An eerie stillness shrouds the night,
Weaves its magic over all.

What stranger comes to steal my sleep?
What ghosts knock at my door?
Are you from a time now hence,
Or have we met before?

They jostled past me one by one
And laughed with cruel derision.
A new fear clutched at my heart
As I watched my ghostly vision.

I recognised them one by one
As they danced before the flames.
With aching heart, I let them depart;
Sweet illusion were their names.

July 19, 1978

BY MY SIDE

Play that melody again
And sing it soft and low.
Can you feel the passion rising
From all those years ago?

Take my hand and press it close
To the heart that beats for me.
For as long as there is life,
You will be the only love for me.

For many years I have
To break the ties that bind,
To free this captured heart of mine
And another love to find.
And as the years went rushing past,
I was sure that I had won
The battle on my memories.
A new life had begun.

But here you are beside me now,
And time has slipped away,
And you are dearer now to me
Than you were yesterday.

SILENCE

The shadows melt at twilight,
Enfolding day in a velvet gown.
Shadows of majestic purple and gold
Cast their magic on village and town.

Where are all the lonely ones
With heavy hearts and shattered dreams?
Actors playing out their roles;
Life is seldom what it seems.

Too many hearts are aching
In the silence of despair,
And many will cast their burdens aside
When it comes too heavy to bear.

November 30, 1979

A new era has begun with reference to the poet's writing style, which becomes contemplative and looks towards the spiritual meaning of life. The following poems were penned during the eighties, when an individual found inner strength and financial success by holding professional positions in society—hence the word *yuppie*. There were shoulder pads in double-breasted suits, teased hair, and tall fringes to flaunt heavy eye make-up. Punk rock music replaced old, familiar tunes, and the start of computer technology was well underway. However, none of these trends influenced the words scribed on scrap pieces of paper. Rather, the big questions remained, and the search for truth followed.

MY QUESTION

As I sit here in my office—
Medical records, that is—
My mind is working overtime.
I get in quite a tiz.

I gaze at the Compactus,
And the tears begin to flow.
Why, please tell me why
Doesn't anyone know?

The collective human suffering
Contained in all of these files.
Just numbers on brown cardboard.
204 is Ellie Miles.

I ask the learned people
To explain why this is so.
Just God's will, my girl;
We are just not meant to know.

Then wisdom shines upon me
Just like summer rain.
There's not just one amongst us
That qualifies as sane.

LYN BETAR

VALLEY OF MINDS

Dream on, gentle dreamer,
Free from all mortal binds.
Visions pure as that first dawning
Float through the valley of the minds.

Could the spirit shed its shackles
That hover as the beasts of hell
Screaming from abysmal depths
As did the ancient ones foretell

Pass on through the pearly portals.
Serenity as an astral glow,
Floating on nebulous wings
Few mortal souls may ever know.

SEASONS OF CHANGE

Why did summer have to go?
Very soon the winds will blow;
Then comes the ice and snow.

The mornings are extremely dark;
No more trips to the park,
Where our fury friends like to have a bark
And love to leave their special mark.

The lovely gardens have no show;
Temperatures plummet too low.
Why do summer have to go?

PEBBLE ON THE PATH

As day folds into evening
And the hustle and bustle are done,
There's time to sit and ponder
With the setting of the sun

Do you ever ask yourself
About the whys of yesterday
That have led us to this place
As we stumble on our way?

Can you believe there is a meaning
To each pebble on the path?
That every fearful crisis
May have a happy aftermath?

If you believe in magic
And it's for us all to share,
Your heart will be uplifted,
And the burdens lie to bear.

There are so many forms of magic
That are blessings from above,
But the greatest of them all
Is the magic of our love.

LET THE NOW BE EVER PRESENT

I'm the mirror of your soul.
Mould me with your mind, behold.
You will never see perfection
If you never look beyond.

Don't look for things that are not there,
Chasing rainbows in the air.
Glide in wings made out of love.
I'll make it right if you are there.

I'll make your nights feel soft as velvet
And your days full of the sun.
Let the now be ever-present,
For we have just begun.

So let the now be ever-present;
Night and day will be as one.
Heaven's glory for a lifetime,
If you'll only look beyond.

I'll make your night feel soft as velvet
And your days full of the sun.
Let the now be ever-present,
For we have just begun.

Let the now be ever-present,
Yes, for we have just begun.

THE TEMPLAR

The sun now shines upon our face.
The clouds have blown away.
Weary warriors of our lord
Embrace a brand-new day.

The scales have tipped.
The pendulum swings
To lighten all our hearts.
The spirit breaks the fettles
To soar on angels' wings.

The veil is lifting from our eyes;
Blessings shower like rain.
The spectres of a thousand years
March by us once again.

I hear the muffled voices
Saying, Free to rest at last.
Too long were we in purgatory,
Ancestors of our past.

Raise the shield of good endeavour
And behold this wondrous age.
There shall be rejoicing
As we turn the global page.

So meditate on charity
And hope, a little turtle dove.
But the greatest gift
Is a heart that fills with love.

I hear the trumpets blowing
And smell the sweet, soft earth.
I have fought beneath the flag
Of the land that gave me birth.

In the fading moments,
I feel a sense of serene.
In the arms of Jesus,
A templar I have been.

Darkness all around me
In my dying throws.
I long once more to kiss the lips
Of my sweetheart, Rose.

LYN BETAR

BLACK DOG

You visit in the dark of the night,
Always there in the morning light.
You rarely ever leave my side;
We seem to be forever tied.

The clown always has a tear,
For he or she knows what to fear.
Through the shadows we see you creep.
You cannot bear to see us sleep.

We then rejoice at the rising sun,
Another day of hope begun.
But then, alas, through the mist and fog
We see the approach of big black dog.

THE DAY IN THE LIFE OF A FAIRY

I'd like to define my topic.
I believe that's the thing to do.
Is all about some fairy folk
That I want to speak to you.

There's not much research on the subject.
Most people tread very weary.
But I want to enlighten this ignorant group
About the day in the life of a fairy.

You must realise first, however,
They are diverse as the nations on earth
And have their own ethnic subculture
Depending on country of birth.

The fairies of Norway and Sweden
Ugly as a hatful of whatever,
And so appear only now and then.
Trolls are the names of these fairys,
Whose origins are very obscure,
But they hang about the fjords.
Apart from that, they have no allure.

We now move on to Ireland,
Who boast their own kind of fairy.
They inhabit all of that country
From Dublin to Tipperary.

And he is called the leprechaun
And appears both day and night,
And are revered by the Irish.
But we know they're not so bright.

It is considered to be lucky
To catch these little men,
Who will grant your dearest wish
If you let them go again.

England is full of fairies,
And they mostly join the navy,
Scrub the deck, and sing "Blow the Man Down,"
And whose habits are unsavoury

Now, Shakespeare knew some fairies;
To them he devoted a play.
This lot didn't do very much
Except get into mischief all day.

There is another group called gnomes—
Not your garden variety—
Who are fond of the amber ale,
Not noted for their sobriety.

Pixies, gnomes, and gremlins—
How plentiful the list
Who comprise the fairy family.
There's probably some I've missed.

Now, that's enough of the background.
I hope you are all impressed
How I have researched my topic
And that I have not digressed.

Now, the day in the life of a fairy.
I've chosen one that you know
Who works his little wings off
Through rain and wind and snow.

He never takes a holiday;
The demand for his service is great.
And through the busy season,
He employs the help of a mate.

He was a star of a radio show,
Avoided by the weary,
The darling of the breakfast hour:
The incredible tooth fairy.

He flitters around most every night
With only moonlight to find his way
And seeks out little boys and girls
Who has lost a tooth that day.

The tooth is slipped into a glass
At the bedside of her tot,
And it's mothers that I really blame
For all this tommyrot.

Now, our fairy leaves some silver
And takes the tooth away,
And everyone is happy
When the silver is found the next day.
That's the day in the life of a fairy,
And each fact I know is right.
It was told to me by the fairy himself
When I was late home one night.

He met me by the garden gate
When I fell over the cat,
And we sat down by the garbage bin
And had our little chat.

I wasn't feeling very well,
But I don't suffer from delusion.
I'll just leave it up to you
To draw your own conclusion.

The following decade was a time celebrated by people, events, and places. A strong connection to the town in which the poet lived afforded the material for the rich and descriptive selection of poems.

THE ACCOUNTANT

Now that you are over seventy
And the tide has turned,
Past knowledge is now useless;
Forget everything you learned.

And to help you readjust,
I'll give you some advice.
So pay close attention;
I'm not gonna say it twice.

I'm here armed with wisdom,
A fraction older I regret.
And with the passing years,
You won't let me forget.

Your belly will sag to your knees,
Your appendage lost from view,
Never to be seen again,
Very sad but true.

Your hair will quickly disappear
Together with your sight.
And watch that bloody prostrate,
Or you will get an awful fright.

For the lost libido,
Take a little kelp.
You'd know about Viagra,
And splints will often help.

As a social person
Who loves a great venue,
Sadly, your lower back
Will go out more than you.

Then there's the "-itis" family.
Arthur, he's the worst.
Take Osteo twice daily,
But do yoga first.

The above will also help the feet,
Which don't work every morning.
They're connected to the penis,
So you'd better heed my warning.

And for general aches and pains,
When you drink your morning shandy,
If you can remember,
Just add a dash of brandy.

With reference to memory loss,
This must not be missed.
The tablets for Alzheimer's
Are on the freebie list.

When the memory starts to fade
And names become a trouble,
Darling always works quite well
And won't burst your bubble.

I think I've covered everything
Except the facts on scoring.
I'm sure that Tina's mentioned
That you probably find boring.

I do suggest a Vital Call
When you are home alone.
In a sudden crisis,
You won't make it to the phone.

And as the many years roll by,
We wish you heaps of luck.
And when your memory fails,
Hope you remember how to

Be a great accountant!

MARRIAGE OF A MECHANIC

Now that they are married,
These two shall be as one,
Doing life together.
We hope it's mostly fun.

But when the road gets bumpy,
Use love-injected hearts.
And if repairs are needed,
Just use genuine parts.

And with regular service
And lots of aftercare,
After many thousand miles,
There'll be warranty to spare.

Some advice to Robyn
If Andrew's strengths recede:
His toolbox will be handy;
Grab a set of jumper leads.

If this doesn't work
And the problem is much larger,
Forget the jumper leads
And put him on the charger.

If this advice is followed
Without a grizzle or a gripe,
In a year or two
You will have a prototype.

LYN BETAR

CREW OF TWO

Captain Col and fearless Fred,
Without a single care,
Winged their way to Rocky
In Captain Col's Glass Air.

A perfect day for flying,
They did not have a clue
Of the peril that awaited
The courageous crew of two.

The plane began to shudder.
The airport was in sight.
The prop was getting looser;
Those bolts gave up in fright.

"Don't think we're gonna make it,"
Col was heard to say.
But Lady Luck was with them
On this Australia Day.

AN ALTERNATE ATTORNEY

This is said with gratitude,
Which sounds like a platitude.
But surely as I write this,
I know that I've become

A literary giant
That can face the defiant,
For a single book for Chrissy
Has changed me from a bum.

So I would like to raise your status;
You could be as great as
Diamond Jim or Perry Mason,
If you have direction.

So please accept this reference
To be treated with some deference.
It will bring you up to date
In striving for perfection.

This gift is sent sincerely
As we regard you dearly
And appreciate your friendship
And lawsuits you've erased.

It's just as old and precious,
Like a case of Reschs
Or a diligent attorney,
And cannot be replaced.

POPPY FRED

As we enter your ashes
In the place that you loved best,
Your loved ones are all gathered
For your last request.

Your ashes just a symbol
Of a life that is no more
But who made every shot possible
And achieved the highest score.

You never lost your zest for life.
Your aim was always true.
And we were blessed to know
You as a friend and father too.

And now your bench is empty;
No need to see the dot.
But every day we knew
You gave it your best shot.

And as we leave you in this place
Under the western skies,
Unforgettable is your memory
And twinkle in your eyes.

MY UNCLE

Now, Uncle Ken, you're eighty,
So many songs unsung,
And proves the age-old adage
Just the good die young.

I've known him since I was born,
And he could tell a tale or two.
Mary, Jane, Elizabeth—
Just to name a few.

You probably heard he travelled
At an early age.
He had to leave the country
To escape the husband's rage.

Then he met our lovely Peg,
Who saved him from all sin.
She did her best, tried really hard,
But couldn't keep him thin.

He likes all kind of music,
From trad jazz to Chopin.
And everyone who knows him
Will say he loves a like man.

He's dealt in stock, bonds, and shares
And done so many courses.
And now he's in his dotage,
He deals in bloody horses.

He's always been hard on me
For smoking all my fags—
Only nervous tension
Cause he sends me all these nags.

Pig, Gertie, Millie, Little Shit,
He's really lost the plot.
Just ask me; I oughta know.
I've got the bloody lot.

Now it's payback time, we say.
This song is in my soul.
For your birthday present,
We give you half of Gertie's foul.

ODE TO MARICA

Now that you have reached fifty,
I've got some news for you.
Now, listen very closely;
Don't rush of to the loo.

This is for your education.
If you know what to expect,
You'll be a bit more stable
And completely wrecked.

It's all downhill, my friend.
I cannot give you cheer.
The devastating changes
That happen in a year.

Your vision will start to fade,
But God's being gentle
So when you strip stark naked,
The sight won't send you mental.

The news is good for Easter:
With advancing craft disease,
You can hide your Easter eggs
Anywhere you please.

LYN BETAR

You'll probably need a hobby
If you beat off each infection.
Something to keep you active,
Like a stamp collection.

When you apply your make-up
And are trying to relax,
Try not to get too stressie
When you're filling in the cracks.

Be careful at the races
When in your hands a glass.
Remember to pat the horse's head
And not the trainer's ass.

Now, just a tip for romance:
When Johnny makes his passes,
Don't let him in the bedroom
Till he takes of his glasses.

Not all the news is ghastly,
And this I must espouse.
I believe there is a vacancy
Down at Bracken House.

FOR AN OLD MATE

Yet another birthday,
Just another one.
You have my deepest sympathy;
It can't have been much fun.

Because you married,
Have been many years,
A lesser woman would have cracked
And spent her life in tears.

Now, I better warn you
Of what now lies ahead,
And I will say it slowly
So you remembered what I said.

Arthritis will shortly set in
In every nook and cranny.
Wrinkles will appear everywhere,
Especially around your fanny.

You'll make ghastly gurgling sounds
Every time you wheeze.
When you think it might improve,
You'll sneeze and sneeze.

LYN BETAR

But if you get rid of Peter,
I suspect you'll need some force.
You could improve your stamina
If you buy a decent horse.

Take cheer, dear heart, do not despair.
This is a most important factor.
In spite all you've suffered,
You have outlived the tractor.

I hope the years will be kind
And you'll have a lot of luck.
And if your memory fails you,
Maybe remember how to …
Talk on the phone.

OUR GEORGE

He never ran a marathon,
Never played for Wests,
Never fielded for Australia
In any of the tests.

He ran a greater race,
Dour stayer to the end.
And of anyone who knew him,
We're proud to call him friend.

Now in quiet reflection
Amidst a new-found grief,
We ponder the loss of a gentleman
Whose stay was all too brief.

He didn't strive for riches,
Did not dream of gold.
His legacy's so lovely,
Just starting to unfold.

His gift is one of hope,
Not to give into despair,
To make the most of every day,
To love, to laugh, to care.

The dignity of grace in his grief
With the loss of his wife and best friend
Is ever a lesson to me
Because life was so sweet to end.

So we reflect on the life of a hero
And the pearls we have received,
And pray for some of his courage
If we are ever in need.

So vale our dear Mr. Monday,
So much for fortune and fame.
We have a shining example
And a racehorse that bears his name.

OL' GRANDDAD

At Wanaaring he was born
In the June of eighty-five.
Life was very different
when Granddad was alive.

He worked on Ellsinora,
Just a stripping lad then.
He loved the outback country,
Where women worked like men.

After the crash of the thirties,
The depression followed on.
All his family had owned
Was completely gone.

The heart-breaking trip to Sydney,
Walking the streets for a job,
Knowing that each day that he
Was part of a growing mob.

The years marched on, however,
When one could best survive.
First memory of my granddad
Was about the age of five.

It wasn't till years later
I realised he was strange.
He never lost the bull dust
From riding on the range.

The old bloke never wore a belt;
Held up his pants with string.
He'd mend a broken chair with wire,
Didn't waste a thing.

When days were cold and windy,
He'd spend some bread with lard,
Build a raging campfire,
Boil his billy in the yard.

He slept on the veranda
Underneath the stars.
I think Nanna kicked him out
With the rest of the galahs.

One morning I remember,
I was barely six.
Granddad roaring like a bull
In an awful fix.

His false teeth were stolen;
They weren't besides his bed.
The kelpie looked so guilty.
That's what Nanna said.

And sure enough, we found them
Beneath the apple tree.
Granddad tried to kick the dog
From Barcaldine to Bree.

I wished we had listened
To the stories he had told then.
Some much history lost
When we buried our old men.

I hope heaven is to his liking
And God is equal to the task,
For no way Granddad's going
Without his whiskey flask.

FRED THE FARMER

Fred the farmer had two sons.
The boys were strong and fit.
The part required for reasoning,
There wasn't much of it.

Fred the farmer didn't know
Which son to leave the farm.
And old Fred was fading fast—
A cause for some alarm.

So Fred devised a little test
And sent them into town.
But first he gave them each a duck
And told them with a frown,

"Go forth and sell your ducks
And be home too late.
Whoever sells his duck for most
Inherits the estate."

The first boy hurried into town
And met an agent there,
Who said, "I'd give you twenty bucks
If you think that fair."

The second boy and his duck
Wandered around in fright
And stood before a darkened door
Of a lady of the night.

The lady said, "It's nice to see
A big, strong lad like you.
But don't let that duck run amok.
It would make a lovely stew."

He said in a flash, "I have no cash,
And my cheque book is in the red."
"Stay a while," said she with a smile.
"I'll take the duck instead."

As soon as Fred knew,
The old boy turned blue
At the fate of his second son,
At the thought of duck stew.
Without much ado,
He reached for his trusty gun.

The moral of this story told
Is each man makes his luck.
Don't leave the straight and narrow,
Or you'll strike out for a duck.

LYN BETAR

DANCING QUEEN

Dear Jean, you are a beauty
I've known you many years.
We've shared a lot of sorrow
And a lot of tears.

I'm very pleased to say
You are such a caring friend
And never waver in your kindness
Till your journey's end.

We've been blessed to know you.
You can really pull a crowd.
Enjoy your lovely family;
You must be very proud.

I'm sure that Noel is with you
On your special day,
And when they raise their glass,
He'll say a quiet hooray!

We admire your spunk and spirit,
And in your darkest hour
You could still smell the roses
And enjoy lovely flower.

Your family has sustained you,
And we wish you all the best.
You gave them everything you had
And passed each and every test.

And when I think of you
And all the years between,
Abba mostly came to mind,
For you are their Dancing Queen.

ELISE

Dear Elise, I cannot say
How much you mean to me.
And on this birthday milestone,
I want to set you free

Of all the misconceptions
That you're heard in the past
About the aging process,
Which happens very fast.

We do indeed become wise,
But no one wants to hear.
That's if you can remember,
And that's the greatest fear.

Your boobs will sag down to your waist,
Can't tie your shoes with ease.
And that is simply because
You can't bend your bloody knees.

Your eyes will dim, your hair turns grey,
You'll dribble from your mouth.
And if that isn't bad enough,
Just watch your arse go south.

There are other pluses.
You don't have to work as hard,
And you'll be really chuffed
When you get your seniors card.

That's all I really want to say.
Hope I've brought you lots of cheer.
Have a happy birthday
And a super awesome year.

LYN BETAR

THE FIRST NOEL

In the shadows of his illness,
When death was by his side,
His spirit rose to meet his God
With dignity and pride.

We hope you know your passing
Has left us with your song.
Gone, but not forgotten,
We'll meet again ere long.

If anyone deserves a place
In God's home up above,
You are there already
Surrounded by our love.

THE ALBUM

Hello, Goochi.
Bless your heart.
Thanks for all you've done.
Apart from other attributes,
The album was great fun.

There's Rick and his mouth,
And Lee looking very pissed.
I was always perfect;
Hope that wasn't missed.

There's Henry and the elephants.
What more can I say?
It was hard to tell the difference
When Henry looked away.

And Carol does a super job,
As good as any fella.
It's neat the way she doubled up
And played the fortune teller.

And it's very democratic
Mike was dealer of the year.
He just slipped John fifty bucks,
Plus a case of beer.

Cheyenne is a lovely girl,
And Steve was very zealous.
They sort of hid away a lot,
But I guess we're only jealous.

The trip was very special,
Friendships extra great.
Hope Mark's done enough this year
To be part of the next year's freight.

DESTINATION OUTBACK

We went on a rally
To see the desert flowers,
But the prettiest sight of all
Was the Tibboburra showers.

Now, Howard is in his Nissan,
Which stuffed him from the start.
He doesn't need a turbo;
He only has to fart.

Jeff, ol' mate, came along as well.
It really was a sin,
Because we moved to Dubbo
To get away from him.

We're glad Rambo came along;
This country's tough at best.
But I noticed every morning
He was greener than the rest.

And Peter the tall chemist,
You know him by description.
Can a man who drinks that much
Dispense a suitable prescription?

And there is outback Jack,
Who likes to sleep beneath the stars.
We should have chucked him out
With the rest of the galahs.

Vince came along as well
Because he knew the route,
But every pub we stayed at,
We had to sweep him out.

Jeff was most embarrassed
He lost his pants, of course.
I don't think he's a gelding—
Looks more like a horse.

Poor old Flash has been defused;
He's definitely Captain Rats.
He ought to give up drinking
And stick to saving cats.

Mark, my friend, had a ball,
Loved all the little chats.
You must know who Mark is;
He's the man with all the hats.

I am sick of Blanchie's stupid jokes.
He's gunna get real lonely
If one more time he says,
"Just have one, one only."

I am awfully glad I took bird.
I will say it once again:
When I look around you lot,
He's the only one that's sane.

We've gone a lot of miles,
And we've talked a lot of shit.
There's not one amongst us
Who'd missed a day of it.

Three cheers, hip hip for Howard,
Scotty, and the crew.
It's been a bloody beauty.
Many thanks to you.

ROTARY RALLY

On the first day of the rally,
Our crewmen said to me,
"Let's have a beer,
Let's have more beer,
And a whiskey by the gum tree."

On the second day of the rally,
Our crewmen said to me,
"We're sick of mince.
Let's do a Vince
And drink whiskey by the gum tree"

On the third day of the rally,
Our crewmen said to me,
"We're sick of snags
And sleeping bags.
Let's drink whiskey up the gum tree."

On the fourth day of the rally,
Our crewmen said to me,
"We're sick of tents,
Can't find the gents.
Let's drink whiskey up the gum tree."

On the fifth day of the rally,
Our crewmen said to me,
"We're sick of each other.
They want their mother,
And they can't find the gum tree."

LYN BETAR

On the sixth day of the rally,
Our crewmen said to me,
"We're sick of closing gates,
We miss our pretty mates.
Let's drink more beer and find the gum tree."

On the seventh day of the rally,
Our crewmen said to me,
"We're sick of Mark's snoring;
It gets real boring.
Let's drink Jack Daniels by the gum tree."

On the eight day of the rally,
Our crewmen said to me,
"We're sick of being broke.
This emu egg's a yoke.
We're sick of grog
And frost and fog
And mince and snags,
But we had a great time by the gum tree."

BAND OF BROTHERS

Now, Rotary is a mystery from a woman's point of view.
It's all masculine tradition; out of nobleness it grew.
A courageous band of brothers devoted to a cause,
With a wonderful constitution and some pretty fine by-laws.

And now we've heard a whisper it's much more like a roar.
The wives and ladies want to join; they're knocking at the door.
I'd love to see the ladies join, one or two at least.
But I'm thinking of their welfare, 'cause the outback is a beast.

And what about the pressure when we have to stay back late,
Making dire decisions in the heat of the debate?
Do we want this for the ladies, these gentle, tender flowers?
The stress, the strain, and collective pain that can last for hours?

I'm sure you'll see my point of view; I think I heard a cheer.
Stuff the bloody cup of tea—I'll have another beer!

THAT COULD BE SEEN AT THE EULO QUEEN

Many nights have come and gone,
And many tales been told
Back in the very early days,
When hopefuls searched for gold.

And the Eulo Queen has seen some sights.
If only these walls could speak
Of the pioneer men and women,
The wild, the strong, the weak.

But the wildest night of all—
And they'll talk of it for years
When all the locals gather
At the Eulo Queen for beers—

Was when the big fellow came to town
In his Toyota with the chook.
He stomped and frothed at the bar
Until the walls all shook.

He wrestled everyone in sight
And drank until he was green.
Struck terror in the hearts of men
That could be seen at the Eulo Queen.

July 1994

CHOOKIE SLIPPERS

We all flew back from Kathmandu;
We did it in a hurry.
Perhaps it was the Alpine air,
But I think it was the curry.

I really miss my elephant;
Friends like that are few.
We will arrive by Qantas.
They'll send the bill to you.

There is another problem.
I pondered what to do
About the boots we trekked in
As they are almost new.

The yak yuk was hard to shift,
The gurney was real handy.
But every time I wear them,
My mates say I look bandy.

Then my prayers were answered,
And we chuckled along out loud.
I opened up my parcel;
Now I am trekking on a cloud.

LYN BETAR

SHIPS OF THE DESERT

We all went on a camel ride
To see the great outdoors,
We camelled here, we camelled there,
And hardly had time to pause.

We saw the Olgas, we saw the rock,
And the hours came to pass.
But mostly all we saw
Was the other camel's ass.

All the camels were quite pretty
And loved a little smooch.
And this was quite acceptable—
Till Gonzo spat at Gooch.

Now, Goochie is real sensitive,
A softie to the core.
So only very few will know
Why the Rav camel is no more.

OFFICE PARTY

Well, as you know, it's Christmas.
A time of fun and cheer,
A time to count our blessings
And reflect the passing year.

A time to think of friends
And enjoy what we have done.
To hope the year ahead
Is kind to everyone.

Hope Spare Parts and Service
And the salesmen can be mates.
Hope Lindsay gets enough to eat
And improves his interest rates.

Hope Barb, who's newly marriage,
Doesn't come undone
And doesn't take too serious
What's poked at her in fun.

Tim's away on annual leave,
But we really shouldn't mind.
If he'd have come tonight,
He would have talked us blind.

Phil Dwyer has been published;
He's written a great book
Called *Dealing with Public*.
But sales have been real crook.

Gary has taken over spares;
He's not too bad a bloke.
But I don't visit Phil or Steve
'Cause I'm not allowed to smoke.

And Jeff, may your computer
Be always loyal and true
And never give her password
To anyone but you.

Gloria Marshall has gone broke
And lost everyone's approval.
Now it's Phil McCracken Weight Loss Centre
And place of hair removal.

Tom need never worry;
His future is assured
As director of Macquarie Inn
And chairman of the board.

Andrew's job is service;
He needs all of his resources.
And since he's married Robyn,
He is always doing courses.

Neil McFarrell is a gentle man,
One of nature's best.
A man of many talents
A friend above the rest,

A man of wit and humour
And puns I adore.
But send him to the rego
When it's ten to four.

He's a man of even temper,
The best of any bunch.
But God help us if he sees me
Sneaking Judy out to lunch.

Well, I haven't mentioned Mark.
It's enough I have said.
Merry Christmas to you all.
I'll quit while I'm ahead.

RETIREMENT IS CLEAR

The night too quickly passes by,
And we are growing old.
With apologies to Lawson,
We've had some days of gold,

When Neil swept up the crickets
And all the bugs around here,
And Judy made the rissoles
And helped us drink the beer.

And now that Neil is leaving,
Who will lighten up our day
With puns, quips, and poetry
That helped us on our way?

And who will cook the barbecue
And put Mark in his place?
And who will do the regos now?
We'll miss Neil's pretty face.

Now Tim is Neil's apprentice,
And I'm sure you'll all agree
That Tim had better quickly learn
To write some poetry.

I think Mark's pleased Neil is leaving;
He thinks it's most unfair
That Neil is nearly sixty-five
And still has all his hair.

So good luck, Neil and Judy.
We await your book with tension.
Especially Toyota Tom,
Who's probably earnt a mention.

But this evening is tinged with sadness
As the day draws to an end.
Old George sits in the shadows
To help farewell our friend.

LYN BETAR

LIFE IN A SWAG

Driving down this lonely track,
Got my swag in the back
Of my pick-up truck,
Feeling outta luck.

Don't know where I'll camp tonight.
Better somewhere outta sight.
Got to try to do some sums
Before the morning comes.

Then I think of you,
The one I left behind.
You are always on mind;
Don't know what to do.

Fireflies buzzing by the lake.
Thinkin' my old heart will break
Takes me back to a state
Forty years ago.

It's far too late
For turning round.
No such thing as
Homeward bound.

Demons always chasing me.
Can't clear my memory
Of all the conflicts I have seen
And places I have been.

Thanks a lot, Uncle Sam.
Left my life in Vietnam.
Now I just travel on
Till my days are gone.

Can't hold back the tears.
So many lonely years
'Cause I loved you so
Forty years ago.

THE CLUB

A gathering, a club, an old friend,
Good mates—I want to cry.
We hung out all together,
Far too young to die.

Great competitors we were
And vied with one another.
But when the scores were counted,
We called each other brother.

We all shot, we laughed, we disagreed.
But when the sun had set
We all shook hands and went our way
Till the next event.

Times all change, and sadly
Nothing stands alone.
Ray Johnson will be sadly missed,
Another name upon the stone!

As time passes, so do our insights to view the greater picture. The next section of poems are reflective and profound, and they carry the wisdom only experience can acknowledge.

WISE WORDS ON MARRIAGE

I cannot find the words
To say how much you mean to me.
On this our special day,
I hope you will agree.

We've had our ups and our downs,
Some joys and some sorrow.
But when the dawn has broken,
We've found a brighter tomorrow.

Marriage is a mixture
Of guidance from above.
But the best ingredient is
Hearts so full of love.

MILESTONE

Congratulations, happy birthday.
What a great milestone.
You've put up with an awful lot,
And we never heard you moan.

Keeping controlled all these years,
Even in times of grief,
Not to mention tears
And times of fun and mischief.

Our dear friend,
You look as good as new.
Have a few good vinos;
Can only have too few.

So keep doing what you're doing;
It really works for you.
You are amazing lady
And loved by all you knew.

TWO-DAY RULE

The candles are lit.
It's a wonderful sight.
Presents are wrapped.
The tree is really bright.

The house is all clean
And very nice looking.
But, mate, let me tell you
I'm over the cooking.

The grandkids descend
Like a plague of grasshoppers.
They make such a mess,
You should call the coppers.

You need fifty-five towels
For two days as a rule,
Which doesn't include
The towels for the pool.

Five hundred glasses
Are left on the sink,
And cups, plates, and cans—
It drives you to drink.

You are stuck in the kitchen
From morning to night
While everyone else
Beams with delight.

But then when they leave
And you've waved them goodbye,
All of your loved ones
Bring a tear to your eye.

And so this is Christmas
And time of good cheer.
Thank God it's only
Once every year!

Next year, I will be wiser,
My cause I espouse.
We are doing Christmas
At a younger kid's house

SO, THIS IS CHRISTMAS

So, this is Christmas.
It comes round again.
No peace on this earth
Or goodwill to men!
So we have learnt nothing
And still waging wars.
No end in sight,
And not a just cause!
So let's raise our glasses
And enjoy a good beer,
And toast all our friends
And wish them good cheer!
I'm loving Christmas,
Can't wait for the day.
Tinsel and lights
That brighten the way.
I've locked up the Weber,
Cleaned up the house.
Nothing will stir here,
Not even a mouse!
No hordes of grandkids
Who yell day and night.
No sticky fingers
Because we've seen the light.
After thirty-four years
Of the cooking and fuss,
We've finally worked out
Our kids can feed us.

MOTHER'S WISH

May you always walk in sunshine.
May good fortune be your friend.
May your road be long and happy.
May you reach your journey's end.
May you not meet pain and sadness.
May all your friends be loyal and true.
May your days be strewn with gladness.
This is your mother's wish for you.

LYN BETAR

SONG FOR A SON

Thinking about my father,
Wondering where you are.
But knowing you are near to me
When I pick up my guitar.

Knowing you're a major part
Of the music I create.
Wising you could hear the riffs,
And I'm thinking it's too late.

Then I feel you near,
I hear you sigh.
Just wanna cry for the years
That we let by.

Then I've become a man
With children of my own,
And I truly know
They are just on loan.

Don't know how to tell you
That I miss you so.
Shoulda told you that
Many years ago.

But you are part of me
And everything I do.
Your blood runs through my veins
And my children too.

That's just the way it is.
Most sons will say the same.
I do know your love was true,
And it's not a blaming game.

KARMA, KARMA

It's just so nice to see you all,
Dear, kind, lovely friends.
Mishy must be really chuffed,
But I'll tell some odds and ends.

As lovely as she is now
And a gracious soul,
She started life precocious,
A naughty little troll.

If she thinks Mac
Gives her lots of grief,
She out-bested her
Far beyond belief.

It's just simply karma,
The turning of the wheel.
Now she knows exactly
How I used to feel.

I remember vividly
One day she had a shower,
Yelling, "Come and dry me, Mum."
Alas, I lost my power.

I said, "You can dry yourself.
I am doing something too."
She said, "I will yell and scream
Till I make you do."

She disappeared one day;
It wasn't very funny.
Then rang me from Queensland
And said, "Can you send me some money?"

She climbed out her bedroom window
On another night,
Met friends at the local pool,
Gave me such a fright.

They scaled the fences
As the pool was locked,
Swam their little hearts out.
Believe me, I was shocked.

So many funny stories
That remain untold.
But today we toast our Mish,
Who has a heart of gold.

And I stand before you,
Hair as white as snow.
But I wouldn't change a thing
Over fifty years ago

So let us charge our glasses,
We either wine or beer,
And get up of our arses
And give her a mighty cheer.

MY SONG

Thinking about the children
I've had in my life.
I have been a mother,
And I've been a wife.
It doesn't always work the way
That you dreamed it would,
Married for a lifetime
Like you hoped you would.
We've lost the dreams,
So it seems.
Must make amends
Before our journey ends.
So we find another
Searching for the one,
Never looking back
On the things
That we have done.
It's time to think about
The choices that we make
And think about our children.
For goodness' sake,
Living is not just about
Fortune, fame, and greed.
Check in with your soul
To see what you need.
It's all about forgiveness,
Starting with yourself,
And looking inward
To find your greatest wealth.
So I've sung my song
Looking to the night.
What is done is done.
Hope some things were right.

SWEET MEMORIES

I was sitting by the ocean,
Simply musing on the day.
The glorious sun was rising,
Mist drifting on the bay.

The bird life was arousing
To greet the new warm day.
Then the mist enclosed me
To transport to yesterday.

In the mist a vision
Of you and me at play,
Being young and happy
With a dream for every day.

How we cherish the memories,
And how naïve we were.
Full of hope and wistfulness,
Not knowing what would be.

The years went rushing by us,
And we lost the sense of self,
Also trust and faith,
hope, belief, and health.

Then the mist just parted.
The sun emerged so bright.
Holding hands and crying
Looking to the light.

No one can change the past.
We can but learn, survive.
Wisdom comes with age.
We will keep our dreams alive.

THREAD OF AGES

I saw this card; it came to me.
Is this the thread of ages?
And look upon our book of life
As we turn the yellow pages.

How many stitches have you plied
Over how many years?
How many hopes, how many dreams,
And how many tears?

The ball of wool is like one's life
As it unravels,
Representing the soul's journey
And the astral travels.

So when you hold your needles
And the crochet hook,
It's just like you are writing
Your very own life's book.

Enjoy the passing years
And every moment treasure,
And when you hold your ball of wool,
Know you have got its measure.

ENDURE FOR EVERMORE

The leaves are rustling by the bridge.
Is this the span of ages?
Sunlight sparkling on the ridge,
Ink fading on the pages.

Gaze into the limpid pool
Nestled by the shore.
Memories of a thousand lives
Endure for evermore.

Shine your light on us today.
The wind calls out our names.
We pray to look upon his face
In the candle flame.

The wilderness has been our home.
Our souls ache to be free.
And when the crystal curtains close,
Please takes us home to thee.

DAY'S END

A twilight meets the velvet night.
I like to sit and muse
On the beauty of all nature
We don't too oft peruse.
The wonder of the setting sun,
The brilliance of the hues
As they sparkle on the waters,
The orange, reds, and blues.
The rising of the goddess moon,
Such fantasies of light
Cascading with its beauty,
Heralding the night.
Ah, the beauty of the land,
A kaleidoscope surreal.
The creation of great spirit,
Intangible but real.
The wondrous beauty of the stars,
And I believe it's right.
Just openings in heaven's door,
Letting out the light.
Artemis, weave your magic
On all of God's creation,
Awakening your spirit
Across every nation.
Reclaiming our gratitude,
Let the seeds of love be planted.
Let nothing in our cosmos
Be so taken for granted.

THE OLD MILL POND

Trying to recall
The dreams of ages past,
Glimpsing for a moment,
But the clarity won't last.
Looking backwards through the mist,
Hoping I will find
Shadowy visions and lost dreams
Swirling round my mind
Late one night, a moonlit night.
Crept through an open door,
Tiptoed down the garden path
I'd never trod before.
The dewy grass like new mown hay.
The roses on the vine.
Childlike voices on the breeze—
Have you come to play?
Gazed into the old mill pond.
The reflection was not me.
A little girl from ages past
As sad as she could be.
She spoke softly through her tears.
"I see your dreams have flown.
Life can be hard at best,
But you are not alone."
Clouds came across the moon
And left an afterglow.
Alas, that little girl was me
Seventy years ago.

LOST SOUL

Its nine o'clock on a Saturday.
Oh God, how I love that song!
Just minding my own effin' business,
Don't want to do anything wrong.

Okay, I drank a bottle of gin;
Was feeling a little bit sad.
He just pissed me of with his blasphemy.
Could feel myself getting so mad!

I've tried so hard to be straight down the line.
Why can't they leave me just be?
The voices are sending me crazy,
Forever taunting and tormenting me.

I reach again for the bottle.
Once more I have succumbed to the shame.
Used up all my excuses;
Not one person left I can blame.

And the nightmare continues.
Why won't the pain go away?
Dirty, dissolute, down on my knees,
And lost the power to pray.

Ah, I think I hear angel voices
Coming to take me away.
The faintest prick of a needle,
And, alas, the dawning of day.

LYN BETAR

THE JOURNEY

I see as if I'm dreaming:
The ebbing of the tide,
The sunset on the water.
Yet I know I must abide.

A journey still awaits us,
Still many a twist and turn
Before the angel's voices beckon,
So many tasks to learn.

Our steps will often falter
Before our tolling bell.
With hope, we pray that God will say,
"You've done your life's work well."

HALCYON DAYS

The ocean crashing on the shore.
Hear the ship bells ringing
Far across the ragged cliffs,
Hear the seabirds singing.
Skies melt into the sea
Midst the furious foam.
My spirit soars on wings above;
I have no other home.
Where are the creatures of the deep,
Untouched by human hand,
Echoes of a distance past
From some other land?
Blessed are the souls who seek
To knock on heaven's door.
Blessed are these gentle souls,
The meek, the lame, the poor.
We must speak in tongues
In gratitude and praise.
Life is all illusion,
And these are halcyon days.

Printed in the United States
By Bookmasters